WHAT DO YOU KNOW ABOUT

Child abuse

PETE SANDERS and STEVE MYERS

COPPER BEECH BOOKS
BROOKFIELD, CONNECTICUT

Designed and produced by
Aladdin Books Ltd
28 Percy Street
London W1P 0LD

First published in the United States
in 1996 by Copper Beech Books,
an imprint of The Millbrook Press
2 Old New Milford Road
Brookfield, Connecticut 06804

Printed in Belgium

Design   David West
                Children's Book
                Design
Editor   Sarah Levete
Picture research Brooks Krikler
                Research
Illustrator   Mike Lacey

Library of Congress Cataloging-in-Publication Data

Sanders, Pete.
Child abuse / Pete Sanders and Steve
Myers.
p. cm. -- (What do you know about)
Includes index.
Summary: Discusses child abuse and the
different forms it takes, as well as why
some people become abusive, and the
effects of abuse on both the victims and
those close to them.
ISBN 0-7613-0488-6 (hardcover)
1. Child abuse--Juvenile literature. 2.
Abused children--Juvenile literature. 3.
Abusive parents--Juvenile literature. [1.
Child abuse.] I. Myers, Steve. II. Title. III.
Series: Sanders, Pete.
What do you know about.
HV713.S25   1996
362.7'6--dc20   95-42435
                          CIP
                          AC

CONTENTS

HOW TO USE THIS BOOK
The books in this series are intended to help young people to understand more about issues that may affect their lives.

Each book can be read by a child alone, or together with a parent, teacher, or helper. Issues raised in the storyline are further discussed in the accompanying text, so that there is an opportunity to talk through ideas as they come up.

At the end of the book there is a section called "What Can We Do?" This gives practical ideas which will be useful for both young people and adults. Organizations and helplines are also listed, to provide the reader with additional sources of information and support.

INTRODUCTION

MOST PEOPLE WOULD NEVER DREAM OF CAUSING DELIBERATE HARM OR
UNHAPPINESS TO A CHILD OR YOUNG PERSON.

**Unfortunately, many children and young people live in situations
where they are subjected to abuse.**

This book explains what child abuse is, and the different forms it can take. Each
chapter introduces a different aspect of the subject, illustrated by a continuing
storyline. The characters in the story have to deal with situations which many
people may face at some point in their lives.

  After each episode, we stop and look at the issues raised, and broaden the
discussion. By the end, you will know more about child abuse, why some people
become abusers, and the effect that abuse can have both on victims and those
close to them.

WHAT IS CHILD ABUSE?

EVERY YOUNG PERSON HAS THE RIGHT TO GROW UP WITHOUT BEING HARMED BY OTHERS, AND TO HAVE HIS OR HER BASIC NEEDS MET.

However, there are people who choose to ignore the rights and feelings of children.

To abuse someone means to mistreat or harm that person deliberately, either physically or mentally. Everyone gets hurt now and again, and this may sometimes be as a result of the action of somebody else. But being hurt by accident is very different from being deliberately abused.

There are four different kinds of abuse. These are physical, emotional, and sexual abuse, and neglect. Sometimes young people are subjected to more than one kind of abuse at the same time. It may happen just once, or it may go on for a long time – perhaps for many years. Some people believe that certain forms of abuse are more serious than others. However, it is important to remember that all forms of abuse are wrong and that they are never the fault of the person who is being abused.

Every child and young person has the right to be protected and loved. No form of abuse is acceptable.

▽ Laura Swann and her friends had gone to the park to play after school one afternoon.

▽ Fatima and Stuart went over to Laura.

◁ Laura was upset. Before the others could stop her, she ran off into the park.

15 MINUTES LATER...

◁ They searched for Laura for awhile. There was no sign of her. They decided she had made her own way home.

▽ When Laura arrived at school the next day, her friends were waiting for her.

▽ Tim came across and apologized to Laura.

Fatima is worried about being late.
Each family is unique. Not all parents and guardians have the same ideas about discipline. Some believe in being strict; others might be more easygoing. They may be influenced by particular cultural or religious beliefs. Most parents' and guardians' attitudes toward discipline are formed because of their concern for the well-being and safety of their children.

Laura has run off to the woods alone.
Child abusers may take advantage of isolated and dark places so it is important to be sensible about where you go. Always use well-lit paths and if possible walk with a group. Although most abuse is carried out by people known to the child, never accept a ride from or go off with a stranger, even if he or she knows your name or claims to be a friend of someone you know.

Many parents and guardians have rules which they expect children to follow.
These can seem unfair, particularly if you feel you should be allowed more freedom to decide for yourself.

One common rule involves being home by a certain time. Usually this is because parents and guardians want to be sure that their children are safe. If you are going to be late, phoning home can save a lot of worry, and is a responsible and adult thing to do.

PHYSICAL ABUSE AND NEGLECT

PHYSICAL ABUSE IS AN ACTION WHICH INTENTIONALLY CAUSES HARM TO A YOUNG PERSON'S BODY. NEGLECT IS THE FAILURE OF PARENTS OR GUARDIANS TO MEET A YOUNG PERSON'S BASIC PHYSICAL AND EMOTIONAL NEEDS.

Physical abuse may take the form of hitting, kicking, punching, biting, scratching, shaking violently, or even burning. It can also mean giving a child dangerous drugs or poisons.
Young people have suffered terrible and even fatal injuries as a result of physical abuse. Their bones may have been broken, or they may have been burned with cigarettes. Not all abuse is this severe. Some children are physically abused for years without their injuries needing special treatment, although they might frequently have cuts and bruises which they try to explain.

Neglect can mean that a young person is not given enough food, is kept in the cold or dark, or is left alone for a long time. It could be that parents do not obtain medical help when the child needs it.
Neglect is being deprived of the things which are essential to our physical and emotional well-being. It does not mean being denied everything we want! In extreme cases of neglect, children have starved to death because they have not been fed, even though the parents or guardians themselves may have eaten well. Or the children may have been left to look after themselves.

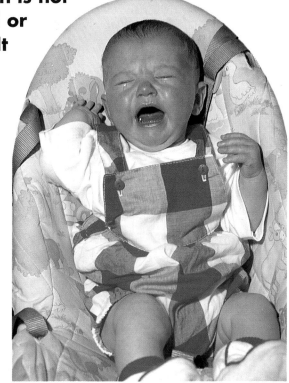

Some children have been left for hours, or even days, without the care they need.

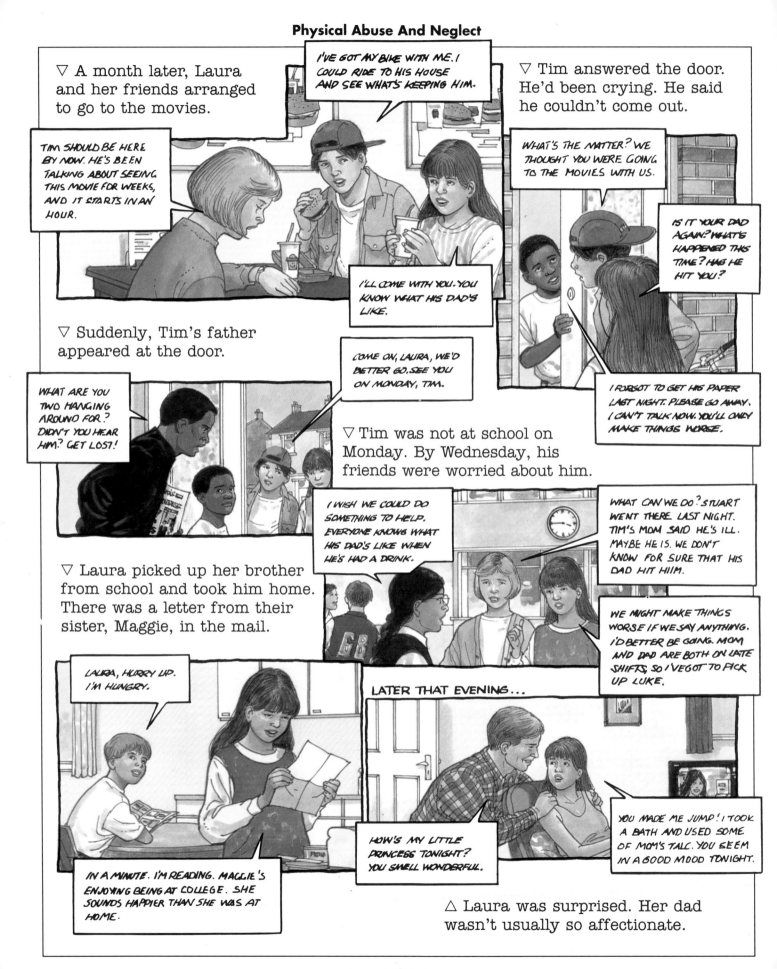

▽ A month later, Laura and her friends arranged to go to the movies.

I'VE GOT MY BIKE WITH ME. I COULD RIDE TO HIS HOUSE AND SEE WHAT'S KEEPING HIM.

TIM SHOULD BE HERE BY NOW. HE'S BEEN TALKING ABOUT SEEING THIS MOVIE FOR WEEKS, AND IT STARTS IN AN HOUR.

I'LL COME WITH YOU. YOU KNOW WHAT HIS DAD'S LIKE.

▽ Tim answered the door. He'd been crying. He said he couldn't come out.

WHAT'S THE MATTER? WE THOUGHT YOU WERE GOING TO THE MOVIES WITH US.

IS IT YOUR DAD AGAIN? WHAT'S HAPPENED THIS TIME? HAS HE HIT YOU?

I FORGOT TO GET HIS PAPER LAST NIGHT. PLEASE GO AWAY. I CAN'T TALK NOW. YOU'LL ONLY MAKE THINGS WORSE.

▽ Suddenly, Tim's father appeared at the door.

WHAT ARE YOU TWO HANGING AROUND FOR? DIDN'T YOU HEAR HIM? GET LOST!

COME ON, LAURA, WE'D BETTER GO. SEE YOU ON MONDAY, TIM.

▽ Tim was not at school on Monday. By Wednesday, his friends were worried about him.

I WISH WE COULD DO SOMETHING TO HELP. EVERYONE KNOWS WHAT HIS DAD'S LIKE WHEN HE'S HAD A DRINK.

WHAT CAN WE DO? STUART WENT THERE LAST NIGHT. TIM'S MOM SAID HE'S ILL. MAYBE HE IS. WE DON'T KNOW FOR SURE THAT HIS DAD HIT HIM.

WE MIGHT MAKE THINGS WORSE IF WE SAY ANYTHING. I'D BETTER BE GOING. MOM AND DAD ARE BOTH ON LATE SHIFTS, SO I'VE GOT TO PICK UP LUKE.

▽ Laura picked up her brother from school and took him home. There was a letter from their sister, Maggie, in the mail.

LAURA, HURRY UP. I'M HUNGRY.

IN A MINUTE. I'M READING. MAGGIE'S ENJOYING BEING AT COLLEGE. SHE SOUNDS HAPPIER THAN SHE WAS AT HOME.

LATER THAT EVENING...

HOW'S MY LITTLE PRINCESS TONIGHT? YOU SMELL WONDERFUL.

YOU MADE ME JUMP! I TOOK A BATH AND USED SOME OF MOM'S TALC. YOU SEEM IN A GOOD MOOD TONIGHT.

△ Laura was surprised. Her dad wasn't usually so affectionate.

Laura and her friends know that Tim's father beats him.
They believe that they cannot do anything about it because they are not adults, and that to become involved would only make things worse. It can be difficult to know what to do to help in this situation. But if you do suspect that another young person is being abused, it is important to talk to an adult whom you trust. He or she may be able to do something about what is going on.

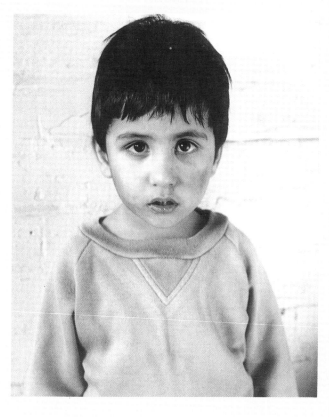

Some people believe that smacking is an effective form of punishment.
Usually a smack is meant as a reminder that the child has done something wrong, and is a warning not to do it again. But some people disagree with any form of physical punishment. Others say it is not harmful, saying it does not do any lasting damage to the child.

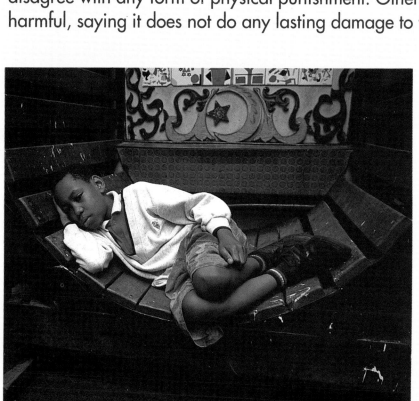

Laura is experiencing some neglect.
She is still young, but because her parents have to work long hours, Laura has to pick up her brother from school, let herself into the house, and make dinner for them both. Although it is illegal in some countries for children below a certain age to be left alone in the house, many young people are in the same situation as Laura. Sometimes this is because there are financial pressures on the parents.

EMOTIONAL AND SEXUAL ABUSE

EMOTIONAL ABUSE MEANS UNDERMINING A YOUNG PERSON'S SELF CONFIDENCE AND EMOTIONAL WELL-BEING. SEXUAL ABUSE MEANS TAKING ADVANTAGE OF A YOUNG PERSON IN A SEXUAL MANNER.

Emotional abuse can involve continually ignoring a child, not showing any love or affection, or constantly ridiculing him or her. Children who are emotionally abused are often told that they are not loveable. They will not be praised or offered any encouragement. To the child, the abuser will often seem to be two different people – nice one minute and nasty the next. This can be very confusing for the young person.

Sexual abuse can mean forcing a young person to take part in sex acts. Or it may be inappropriate touching of the child's body. Sexual abuse imposes adult experiences on a child before he or she is physically or emotionally ready for them. An abuser might ask children to touch parts of his or her body, or show them lewd pictures or videos. The behavior of the abuser may at first appear innocent, and the young person might not realize what is happening.

Emotional abuse may involve a young person being criticized, taunted, or humiliated, sometimes in front of other people.

▽ A few days later, Laura's mom was getting ready to go to work.

WHEN CAN I HAVE MY NEW SNEAKERS, MOM? PAT'S GOT SOME, AND YOU PROMISED I COULD HAVE A PAIR TOO.

LAURA, I'M DOING MY BEST. I DON'T THINK YOU UNDERSTAND HOW MUCH THINGS COST, SOMETIMES.

YOU KNOW I DO, DARLING. NOW LAURA, YOUR DAD SHOULD BE BACK BY NINE O'CLOCK. MAKE SURE LUKE'S IN BED BY THE TIME HE GETS HOME.

DO YOU HAVE TO WORK LATE AGAIN, MOM?

I ALWAYS DO, DON'T I?

▽ When her dad arrived home, Laura told him about the sneakers, and what her mom had said.

▷ Mrs. Swann left. Laura felt really miserable.

IT'S NOT FAIR. MOM PROMISED I'D HAVE NEW SNEAKERS NEXT WEEK. NOW WHAT AM I GOING TO DO?

DON'T WORRY, PRINCESS, I'LL SEE WHAT I CAN DO. HAVE I EVER LET YOU DOWN YET?

▽ Laura smiled. Her dad went upstairs for a bath.

DO ME A FAVOR, PRINCESS, AND BRING ME UP THE PAPER, WOULD YOU?

OK, I'LL BE UP IN A MINUTE.

▽ By the time Laura went upstairs, her dad was already in the bath.

THANKS, PRINCESS. WHY DON'T YOU COME IN AND TALK TO ME FOR AWHILE.

NOT WHEN YOU'RE IN THE BATH, DAD!

▽ The telephone rang. Relieved, Laura ran to answer it. It was Tim.

ARE YOU OK? WHEN YOU DIDN'T TURN UP FOR SCHOOL, WE WERE ALL REALLY WORRIED. TIM, HAS YOUR DAD BEEN ON YOUR BACK?

YOU DON'T UNDERSTAND. DAD CAN BE GREAT SOMETIMES. IT'S JUST WHEN HE HAS A DRINK, HE GETS INTO THESE TERRIBLE MOODS.

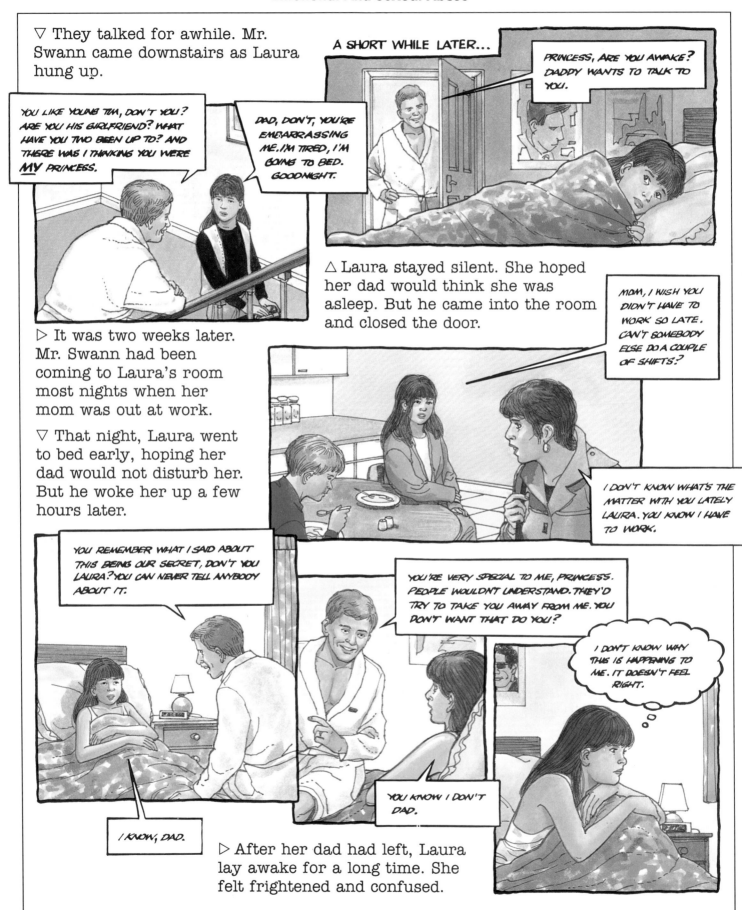

▽ They talked for awhile. Mr. Swann came downstairs as Laura hung up.

YOU LIKE YOUNG TIM, DON'T YOU? ARE YOU HIS GIRLFRIEND? WHAT HAVE YOU TWO BEEN UP TO? AND THERE WAS I THINKING YOU WERE *MY* PRINCESS.

DAD, DON'T, YOU'RE EMBARRASSING ME. I'M TIRED, I'M GOING TO BED. GOODNIGHT.

A SHORT WHILE LATER...

PRINCESS, ARE YOU AWAKE? DADDY WANTS TO TALK TO YOU.

▷ It was two weeks later. Mr. Swann had been coming to Laura's room most nights when her mom was out at work.

▽ That night, Laura went to bed early, hoping her dad would not disturb her. But he woke her up a few hours later.

△ Laura stayed silent. She hoped her dad would think she was asleep. But he came into the room and closed the door.

MOM, I WISH YOU DIDN'T HAVE TO WORK SO LATE. CAN'T SOMEBODY ELSE DO A COUPLE OF SHIFTS?

I DON'T KNOW WHAT'S THE MATTER WITH YOU LATELY LAURA. YOU KNOW I HAVE TO WORK.

YOU REMEMBER WHAT I SAID ABOUT THIS BEING OUR SECRET, DON'T YOU LAURA? YOU CAN NEVER TELL ANYBODY ABOUT IT.

YOU'RE VERY SPECIAL TO ME, PRINCESS. PEOPLE WOULDN'T UNDERSTAND. THEY'D TRY TO TAKE YOU AWAY FROM ME. YOU DON'T WANT THAT DO YOU?

I DON'T KNOW WHY THIS IS HAPPENING TO ME. IT DOESN'T FEEL RIGHT.

I KNOW, DAD.

YOU KNOW I DON'T DAD.

▷ After her dad had left, Laura lay awake for a long time. She felt frightened and confused.

Abusers use different methods to get people to go along with what is happening.

Abusers need to prevent anyone else from finding out about their behavior because they know it is wrong. They will go to great lengths to make sure that the person they are abusing remains silent and keeps their "special" secret. Some abusers will try to bribe a young person, promising gifts or special treats. Others use threats, making the young person believe that the abuse is his or her fault.

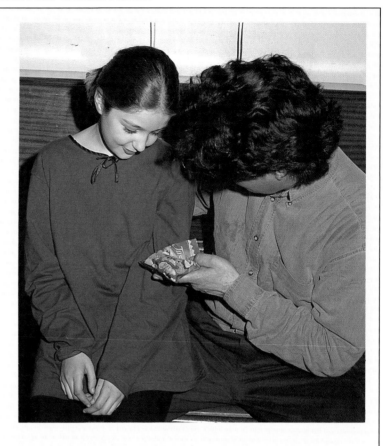

Sexual feelings are perfectly natural.

But it is important that any expression of these is appropriate. It is never acceptable for an adult to take advantage of a young person's curiosity about sex. A child should not feel that his or her own sexual curiosity is to blame for any sexual abuse by an adult.

Laura's dad has told her that what has happened is a secret.

We all have secrets. Revealing a secret someone has asked you to keep might seem like betraying that person. Abusers rely on this. They may frighten the abused person into believing that terrible things will happen if the secret is broken. They may even say that if the young person tells anyone, no one will believe him or her. In fact, this is very unlikely. Most adults will take allegations of abuse very seriously.

WHY DOES IT HAPPEN?

THERE IS NO SIMPLE REASON WHY CHILDREN ARE ABUSED OR WHY PEOPLE ABUSE THEM. CHILD ABUSE CAN HAPPEN TO GIRLS AND BOYS OF ALL AGES, FROM DIFFERENT RACES, RELIGIONS, CULTURES, AND SOCIAL SITUATIONS.

The abuser is usually someone the young person knows and trusts – for instance a parent, another relative, a neighbor, a friend of the family, a babysitter, a guardian, or a teacher.

Drugs and alcohol can affect the way a person thinks and behaves. People may become more violent under their influence, and they have been a factor in some cases of abuse. Some people say that poverty and poor living conditions are contributory factors. Abuse of vulnerable young people may occur when the parent or guardian is unable to cope with his or her own feelings; he or she may take this unhappiness out on the children. Research has shown that people who were themselves abused as children are more likely to become abusers as adults.

Although most child abuse is carried out by someone known to the child, strangers may also abuse children. This is why it is important not to talk to or go off with strangers.

Money worries and poor housing can put a lot of pressure on parents and guardians, especially if they do not have any support to help them cope. But much abuse also occurs in families where money is not a problem.

▽ It was two months later. One evening, after school, Tim saw Fatima being bullied by two other girls.

▽ The two girls let Fatima go. Fatima said they had been making fun of her.

HEY, WHAT DO YOU THINK YOU'RE DOING? LEAVE HER ALONE.

YOU STAY OUT OF THIS. IT'S NONE OF YOUR BUSINESS.

LOOK I'VE GOT TO GO. I CAN'T BE LATE OR I'LL BE IN TROUBLE AGAIN. ARE YOU SURE YOU'RE OK, THOUGH?

SHE'S OUR FRIEND. THAT MAKES IT OUR BUSINESS.

NO HE'S NOT. WHAT DO YOU KNOW ABOUT IT ANYWAY? MY DAD'S OK. WHAT'S SO SPECIAL ABOUT YOUR PARENTS, ANYWAY?

YES I'M FINE. YOU GO - DON'T UPSET YOUR DAD AGAIN.

IT MUST BE AWFUL LIVING WITH YOUR DAD. HE'S ALWAYS SO ANGRY.

MY DAD WOULD NEVER TREAT ME THE WAY HIS DOES. HE'D NEVER DO ANYTHING TO HURT ME.

△ Tim was upset and ran off home.

▽ When she had left, Pat said she thought Laura had been acting strangely.

I'VE GOT TO BE GOING. I HAVE TO PICK UP LUKE TONIGHT. SEE YOU LATER.

I'VE NOTICED THAT TOO. SHE'S BEEN KIND OF DISTANT.

▽ At home, Laura made Luke his dinner, and waited for her mom to get home.

PLEASE LET MOM GET HOME BEFORE DAD DOES TONIGHT.

I THINK SHE'S FED UP ABOUT HER PARENTS WORKING ALL THE TIME. SHE ALWAYS ENDS UP HAVING TO LOOK AFTER HER LITTLE BROTHER. IT'S NOT FAIR.

Sometimes children become a "go-between" for their parents. Parents may be so preoccupied with their negative feelings toward each other that they forget about the effects that the situation may be having on their children.

Sometimes, young people may abuse other children. Whoever abuses a child, and whatever his or her reason, it is never acceptable for this to happen.

Abusers can be male or female, young or old, and most look very ordinary. Because there is no one type of person who is more

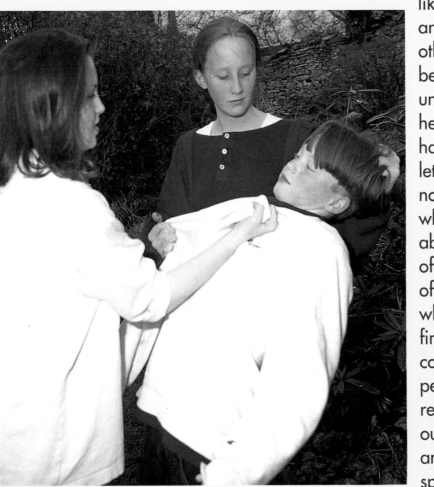

likely to abuse children than another, it can be difficult for others to know that a child is being abused. A child may not understand why those closest to her or him cannot see what is happening. He or she may feel let down because nobody has noticed what is going on. Even when a parent or guardian is abusing a child, other members of the family may not be aware of it. People are usually shocked when abuse is discovered. Many find it hard to accept that abuse could be happening amongst people they know. They may mis-read signs which the child gives out. This is why it is important for anyone who is being abused to speak out about it.

THE EFFECTS OF CHILD ABUSE

ABUSE CAN HAVE A DEVASTATING EFFECT ON PEOPLE'S LIVES, NOT JUST WHILE THEY ARE BEING ABUSED, BUT FOR YEARS AFTERWARD.

The physical effects of abuse, unless an attack has been extremely violent, will usually disappear with time. The emotional turmoil can last much longer.

The effects of abuse will be different in each situation. Children may be confused about what is happening and why, particularly if someone they have loved and trusted seems suddenly to have turned against them. They may feel that nobody can be trusted. They might become more violent when they play. Children who are sexually abused often become obsessed about their bodies and may become sexually aggressive toward other children.

Although it is only the abuser who is at fault, many young people who are being abused feel guilty or "dirty," as if they are doing something wrong. It is important that everyone is aware of how damaging child abuse can be, and learns to understand some of the ways in which young people might express their feelings. Children need to know that there are people they can talk to, and who will believe them.

Young people who are being abused may try to avoid other people as much as possible. They might not want to join in with their friends.

▽ A week later, Laura's teacher asked her to stay behind after class to discuss Laura's schoolwork.

I KNOW YOU CAN DO BETTER THAN THIS LAURA. YOU USUALLY TAKE SUCH CARE WITH YOUR WORK, BUT RECENTLY YOU SEEM TO HAVE LOST INTEREST. YOU'VE STOPPED SPEAKING UP IN CLASS DISCUSSIONS AS WELL.

WHAT'S THE POINT? ANYWAY, IT'S A BORING SUBJECT.

YOU DIDN'T USED TO THINK SO, LAURA. IS SOMETHING WRONG? IF THERE'S A PROBLEM AT HOME, OR ANYTHING YOU WANT TO TALK ABOUT, YOU CAN ALWAYS COME TO ME, YOU KNOW.

NO, EVERYTHING'S FINE. I'VE JUST NOT BEEN FEELING WELL, THAT'S ALL. I'LL DO BETTER, I PROMISE.

△ Laura wanted so much to tell her teacher everything, but she felt too ashamed and confused.

▽ The following Monday was Fatima's birthday. Laura had been invited to her birthday party.

CHEER UP! IT'S SUPPOSED TO BE A PARTY. WHY DON'T YOU COME AND DANCE WITH US?

THAT'S NOT TRUE. WHAT'S WRONG WITH YOU, LAURA? I CAN'T BELIEVE HOW MUCH YOU'VE CHANGED. YOU USED TO BE THE ONE WITH ALL THE FUN IDEAS. NOW YOU JUST MOPE AROUND ALL THE TIME.

WHAT DO YOU CARE? GO AWAY AND LEAVE ME ALONE.

NO, THANKS. I'LL JUST WATCH. I'M A TERRIBLE DANCER ANYWAY.

WAS IT A GOOD PARTY, LAURA? SAY THANK YOU TO FATIMA FOR INVITING YOU. WE SHOULD BE GETTING HOME.

△ Laura was sorry. She apologized to Fatima, and went to dance with the others.

THANKS, FATIMA. I'LL SEE YOU TOMORROW AT SCHOOL.

△ Laura had forgotten what it felt like to enjoy herself. Now she was having a really good time.

▷ Laura's good mood disappeared when the party ended. Her dad came to pick her up.

BYE, LAURA.

18

Child abuse damages a person's feelings of self worth.

Abuse can make young people believe that they do not deserve to be loved. They may begin to hate themselves, and to feel that they should be punished, even though they have done nothing wrong. Children who have been abused may deliberately hurt themselves because they feel so desperate. Some have even tried to kill themselves because the feelings of despair can seem so overwhelming.

The effects of abuse are not always obvious.

People may hide the truth about their feelings for a long time. A young person may try to find other ways of coping with his or her feelings of confusion and anger.

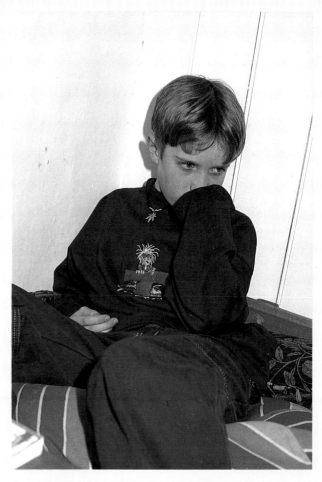

Some young people develop strategies for coping with the abuse.

They might switch off from it, burying emotions which are too painful to face. Or they may even seem to invite the abuse sometimes, preferring that to the constant worry and fear about when, and if, it is going to happen.

Young people may become moody or withdrawn. They may lose interest in their appearance and their schoolwork. Or they may express themselves through violent pictures and aggressive behavior. Sometimes, young people who are being abused will try to attract the attention of other adults by hurting themselves. They want somebody to notice that something is wrong, but are frightened of saying anything.

SHOULD I TELL?

YOU MIGHT THINK THAT IT WOULD BE EASY TO TELL SOMEBODY IF YOU WERE BEING HURT.

Unfortunately, this is not the case for most abused young people. Many are worried about what will happen if they tell. They believe that the consequences could be worse than the abuse itself.

You already know that abusers will go to great lengths to keep the abuse a secret. A parent or close relative who is abusing a young person may have said that telling will cause the family to break up. Children can still love the person who is abusing them, and may feel a sense of loyalty toward him or her. Or they might believe that they themselves will be blamed for causing the abuse in some way. An abused person may not know the right words to express what has been happening. Or he or she may not know who to turn to or might be afraid of not being believed.

People who suspect abuse is going on may also be unsure of what to do to help. They may think "it's none of my business" or "I don't want to get involved." But nobody deserves to be abused. However difficult it may be to tell, abuse should not be allowed to continue. Every child deserves to be protected from abuse.

Being abused by someone trusted, can make it very difficult for young people to trust others. It can take a long time to build up the confidence to tell someone what has happened. But it is a brave and important step to take, and one which will help to stop the abuse.

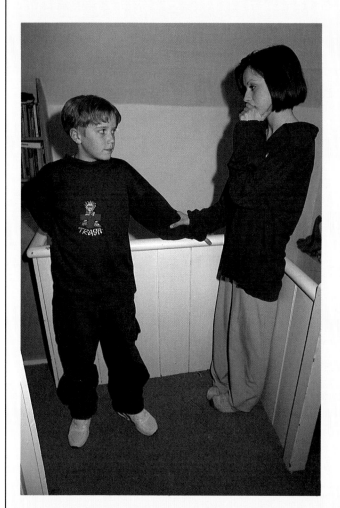

Maggie has discovered that her father has gone on to abuse her younger sister.
She has learned that a person who abuses one child may then do the same to a brother or sister in the same family. This can happen over a long period, without anyone being aware of what is going on, because the abused children have all been sworn to secrecy.

Laura is worried her mom won't believe her.
This fear can make it very difficult to speak out. Most people, however, know that a young person will not accuse someone of abuse unless there is a very good reason, and they will take the statement seriously.

Each abused person's experience will be different.
Some people may be more severely or frequently abused than others. No type of abuse, however, is ever acceptable.

It is very unlikely that the abuse will "go away." Even if it does stop for one person, an abuser, like Laura's father, might eventually be tempted to abuse someone else. This is one reason why it is so important to tell someone you trust about what is happening.

CHILD PROTECTION AND THE LAW

CHILDHOOD IS A TIME WHEN WE LEARN TO MAKE SENSE OF THE WORLD AND WE DEVELOP A SENSE OF OUR OWN IDENTITY.

Child abuse interferes with this process. The laws of most countries recognize this and clearly state that child abuse is a crime. There are procedures laid down to ensure that children are protected. These procedures will differ from place to place, but all put the welfare of the child first. When child abuse is suspected, the police and social services will become involved. They will talk to the child and to the person who is accused of the abuse. If the child is thought to be in danger, they may take her or him out of the home situation. This can be distressing for the child and the family, but they will not be kept apart longer than is necessary. There will also be other legal processes to be

faced. This might mean giving evidence in court. Although it may be frightening and upsetting to have to talk about what has happened, everyone will be making sure that the child suffers as little distress as possible. In some cases, children are allowed to record their evidence on video, so that they do not have to be questioned in court. Sometimes children may use dolls to help them show and explain what has happened to them, if they can't put it into words.

Allegations of child abuse are taken very seriously. Everything will be done to protect the child and to ensure his or her well-being.

▽ The girls spoke to their mom after their dad had left for work. Mrs. Swann was devastated.

I'M SORRY, MOM. I NEVER MEANT THIS TO HAPPEN.

LAURA, NONE OF THIS IS YOUR FAULT. OR YOURS, MAGGIE. I SHOULD HAVE SEEN THAT SOMETHING WAS GOING ON. THIS IS ALL SO DIFFICULT TO TAKE IN.

HOW COULD HE DO SUCH A THING? I'M SO SORRY. WHY DIDN'T YOU COME TO ME BEFORE?

I WANTED TO, MOM, BUT I WAS FRIGHTENED. I LOVED DAD. I COULDN'T UNDERSTAND WHAT WAS HAPPENING. WHEN HE STOPPED, I JUST LOCKED ALL THE BAD FEELINGS AWAY.

I KNOW. WHAT'S GOING TO HAPPEN TO DAD NOW?

▷ Mrs. Swann said she needed some time to think what to do. That afternoon, she called the police.

▽ The police took separate statements from Laura and Maggie.

▽ When Mr. Swann came home from work that evening, the police arrested him.

YOU'VE BEEN VERY BRAVE, LAURA. IT COULDN'T HAVE BEEN EASY TO TELL ME THE THINGS YOU HAVE DONE.

MRS. SWANN, WE NEED TO TALK TO THE GIRLS AT THE POLICE STATION, AND LAURA WILL NEED TO HAVE A MEDICAL EXAMINATION.

THIS IS RIDICULOUS. THERE MUST BE SOME MISTAKE. WHAT HAVE THEY BEEN SAYING ABOUT ME? IT'S ALL LIES. YOU BELIEVE ME DON'T YOU, DARLING?

WHY WOULD YOUR DAUGHTERS LIE ABOUT A THING LIKE THIS? THEY LOVE YOU, AND YOU'VE LET THEM DOWN. SUDDENLY I FEEL AS THOUGH I DON'T REALLY KNOW YOU.

I'LL ARRANGE FOR THEM AND LUKE TO STAY AT MY SISTER'S THIS EVENING.

▽ The next day, the social worker came to see Laura and Maggie at home. She explained what would happen next.

DON'T WORRY. THE COURT WILL DO ALL IT CAN TO MAKE THINGS AS COMFORTABLE AS POSSIBLE FOR YOU. BUT I CAN'T PRETEND IT'S GOING TO BE EASY.

YOU KNOW YOUR DAD'S BEEN ARRESTED. HE'S DENYING THE CHARGES, WHICH MEANS THAT THE CASE WILL HAVE TO GO TO TRIAL.

I CAN'T BELIEVE HE'S ACCUSING US OF LYING.

ALL OF THIS WOULDN'T HAVE HAPPENED IF WE HADN'T SAID ANYTHING.

AND DAD WOULD HAVE GONE ON ABUSING YOU, LAURA. WE'VE DONE THE RIGHT THING.

WILL WE HAVE TO SAY SOMETHING IN COURT?

◁ Although she still felt guilty, Laura knew that what Maggie said was true.

It can be tempting to think that, once the abuse is discovered and stopped, life will immediately return to normal.

However, this is not the case. As the social worker has told Laura, there are still going to be hard times to face. Some children might be tempted to give up, but Laura understands why she must continue. She feels that nothing she has to go through will be worse than the abuse she has suffered.

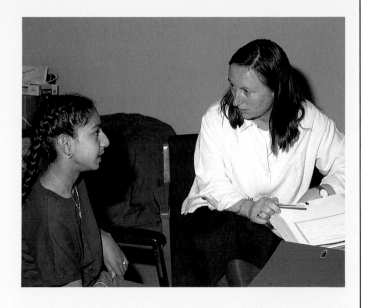

Maggie and Laura's dad has denied the allegations of abuse.

Most abusers do not readily confess to their behavior. Because the legal process gives everyone the chance to have a say, this may mean that the children will have to hear their abuser deny the allegations.

It is very difficult to listen to someone who you may still care about telling lies about you, and refusing to own up to what he or she has done. However, the courts will do everything they can to make the process as comfortable as possible for the child.

Abusers cannot be allowed to continue with their actions.

People have different ideas about what should happen to people who abuse young people. The decision usually depends on the individual case. Some abusers are sent to prison. Others may undergo therapy, where they are helped to think through what they have done and to change their behavior.

FACING UP TO CHILD ABUSE

CHILD ABUSE IS A SUBJECT WHICH MANY PEOPLE DO NOT LIKE TO TALK ABOUT. MANY PEOPLE PREFER TO THINK THAT IT DOES NOT HAPPEN, OR THAT IT COULD NEVER AFFECT THEM OR ANYONE THEY KNOW.

Facing up to child abuse is not easy for anyone. But ignoring the problem will not make it go away.

The law recognizes that child abuse is wrong. However, the legal process only begins when the abuse is discovered. The abuse has already happened; the child will already have suffered emotional or physical cruelty. Until we all confront the problem, children will continue to be abused.

It is important to believe a young person's statement, however incredible it may seem at the time. It is also vital to keep everything in perspective, so that any cases which might turn out not to be abuse are handled sensitively and quickly. In such instances, the child may need help and attention, to discover why he or she made the allegation in the first place.

Abusers may say that they know what they did was wrong, but they couldn't help it. In such cases they may also need help, to make sure that they never abuse anyone again.

It is important to educate both children and adults, informing them about abuse and about the ways in which they can help to keep themselves safe.

▽ Mr. Swann eventually confessed. He went to prison for four years. A year after the case, Laura and Maggie were still seeing a therapist to talk about how they felt.

I STILL KEEP THINKING THAT LAURA WOULD HAVE BEEN ALL RIGHT IF I HAD SAID SOMETHING SOONER.

IT'S SO DIFFICULT TO TALK ABOUT, EVEN NOW. I KEPT IT INSIDE FOR SO LONG. PART OF ME LOVES HIM, BUT I HATE HIM FOR WHAT HE DID.

THAT'S NATURAL. IT'S VERY CONFUSING HAVING LOVING AND HATING FEELINGS LIKE THAT. THERE ARE SOME GOOD THINGS ABOUT YOUR DAD, BUT WHAT HE DID TO YOU WAS WRONG. WHAT ABOUT YOU, LAURA?

YOU CAN'T THINK LIKE THAT, MAGGIE. IT'S NOT YOUR FAULT.

I DON'T KNOW IF I'LL EVER FEEL THE SAME WAY ABOUT HIM AGAIN. HE MADE ME FEEL SO GUILTY AND ASHAMED. I USED TO THINK I DID SOMETHING TO MAKE IT HAPPEN.

MOM'S SEEN HIM, BUT I CAN'T YET. ACTUALLY, MOM'S BEEN TERRIFIC THROUGHOUT THIS WHOLE THING. SHE WAS THE ONE WHO HAD TO EXPLAIN EVERYTHING TO LUKE.

YOUR DAD'S IN A SPECIAL PROGRAM NOW. THEY'RE TRYING TO HELP HIM. HE SAYS HE FEELS SORRY FOR WHAT HE DID, AND WANTS TO SEE YOU. HOW DO YOU FEEL ABOUT THAT?

▽ Laura's family had moved after the trial. Laura was at a new school. One evening, she bumped into Tim.

△ Both girls said it was still too soon for them.

IT'S GOOD TO SEE YOU. HOW ARE THINGS? I HEARD YOUR DAD'S MOVED BACK IN WITH YOU.

I KNOW. I THOUGHT SHE MIGHT BLAME ME FOR WHAT HAPPENED TO DAD, BUT SHE'S BEEN GREAT.

▽ In the end, Laura did decide to go to the party.

THAT'S RIGHT. HE'S STOPPED DRINKING. THINGS ARE MUCH BETTER AT HOME, NOW. EVERYBODY AT SCHOOL KEEPS ASKING HOW YOU ARE.

YOU LOOK NICE, LAURA.

I'M GLAD TO SEE YOU LOOKING SO HAPPY. ARE YOU LOOKING FORWARD TO THE PARTY?

IT'S STUART'S BIRTHDAY IN TWO WEEKS. HE'S HAVING A PARTY. WHY DON'T YOU COME ALONG?

MAYBE I WILL. I'D LIKE THAT.

I'M A BIT NERVOUS, BUT IT WILL BE GOOD TO SEE MY OLD FRIENDS AGAIN.

Laura is not sure whether she will be able to forgive her dad.

In time, some people can forgive their abuser. Others may never feel able to do this. People who have been abused will never forget what has happened, but most are able to recover from the experience. This is not an easy process. It can take a very long time. People will need a great deal of help and support from others.

Tim's father is now receiving help to stop drinking.

He has admitted that he has a problem with alcohol, and that he becomes aggressive when he drinks. This is the first step in doing something about it. It may take a great deal of effort for an abuser to change his or her habits, but it can be done.

Every young person and child has rights.

It is up to everyone in society to ensure that children and young people are protected and that they are given the opportunity to develop physically and emotionally in a safe and positive way. Every young person has the right to enjoy life to the fullest.

WHAT CAN WE DO?

HAVING READ THIS BOOK, YOU WILL UNDERSTAND MORE ABOUT CHILD ABUSE AND THE WAYS IN WHICH IT CAN AFFECT PEOPLE'S LIVES.

You will know that no child or young person should have to put up with abuse, and that abuse is never the fault of the child.
If you suspect that abuse is happening, or know for certain that somebody is being abused, you should talk to somebody about it. Choosing the right person is important. Sometimes this might be a member of your family, a teacher, or another older person whom you trust. If you yourself are being abused, remember that it can be stopped. The decision to tell can be a hard one, especially if you have strong feelings for the person who is abusing you, or if you have been sworn to secrecy or threatened. It may lead to some upheaval and may mean facing up to difficult feelings and situations. However, you have the right to be protected from abuse.

National Committee for Prevention of Child Abuse
332 S. Michigan Ave,
Ste. 1600
Chicago, IL 60604-4357
(312) 663-3520

National Safe Kids Campaign
111 Michigan Ave, NW
Washington, DC 20010
(202) 884-4993

ADULTS ALSO HAVE A RESPONSIBILITY. THEY NEED TO LISTEN TO CHILDREN AND TO BELIEVE THEM, EVEN IF WHAT THEY ARE TOLD IS DIFFICULT TO ACCEPT.

Being more aware of the physical and emotional signs of abuse will also help.
Adults and young people who have read this book together may find it helpful to share their views about the issues raised. People who are experiencing abuse, or who would like more information, might like to talk to somebody who has experience in dealing with this kind of situation. The organizations listed below may be able to provide help and support.

Project Cuddle
1075 Corona Lane
Costa Mesa, CA 92626
(714) 432-9681

National Council on Child Abuse and Family Violence
1155 Connecticut Ave, NW
Suite 400
Washington, DC 20036
(800) 222-2000

National Exchange Club Foundation for the Prevention of Child Abuse
3050 Central Ave.
Toledo, OH 43606
(800) 760-3413

American Humane Association Children's Division
63 Inverness Dr. E
Englewood, CO 80112
(800) 227-4645

Child Abuse Listening and Mediation
P.O. Box 90754
Santa Barbara, CA
93190-0754
(805) 965-2376

INDEX

Photocredits
All the pictures in this book are by Roger Vlitos except pages: 1: Mal Bradley;
9 top, 23 bottom: NSPCC.
The publishers wish to acknowledge that all of the photographs taken by Roger Vlitos
in this book have been posed by models.